A long, long time ago, people didn't know what money was.

Back then, people lived in villages. Everyone worked and used what they made to trade with others. For example, Alex was good at picking apples, so he traded his extra apples. Emma was great at fishing, so she traded her extra fish. If Alex wanted fish and Emma wanted apples, they could trade. This type of trading, called "barter," is when you trade things directly.

As people kept trading, they noticed that some rare things were more popular. For example, shiny seashells or precious stones. Almost everyone wanted them, and people were happy to trade their goods for these items. These rare objects slowly started to act as a general trading tool, leading to the creation of money.

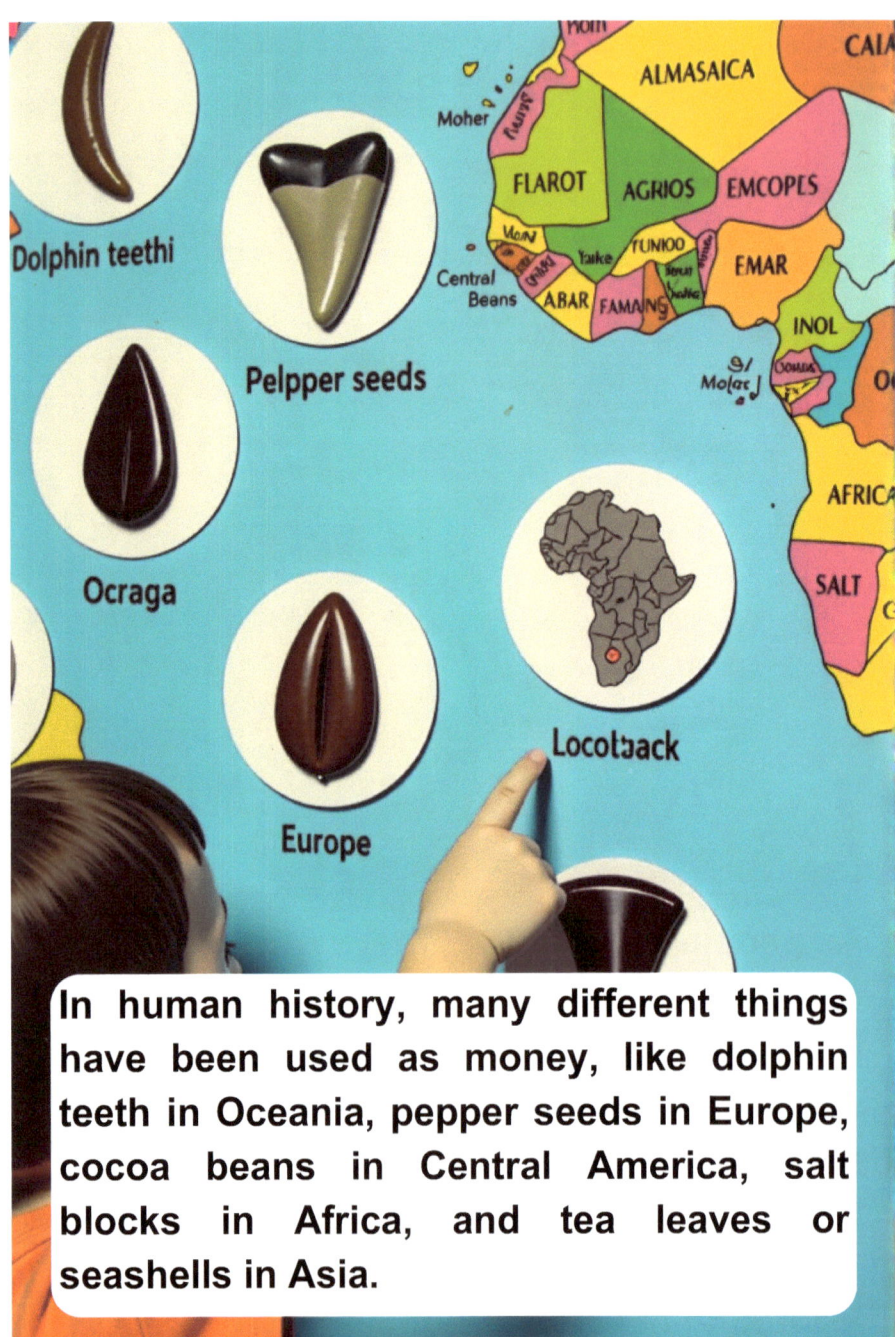

In human history, many different things have been used as money, like dolphin teeth in Oceania, pepper seeds in Europe, cocoa beans in Central America, salt blocks in Africa, and tea leaves or seashells in Asia.

So, these rare items became the first form of money. For example, if you wanted a meet, you might need to give 5 seashells. If you had seashells, you could trade them for what you wanted.

Another problem was that seashells could easily break. If your seashell cracked, who would want to trade for it? This caused trouble during trading.

Also, seashells came in different sizes. Some were big, some were small, but should they have the same value? People often argued about this, which made trading harder.

People started to realize that while seashells were useful, they weren't perfect. They began thinking, "Is there something better we can use instead of seashells?" This question puzzled people for a long time. They began searching for a better solution and eventually turned to metal.

About 2,700 years ago, people began using gold, silver, and bronze to make coins of different sizes and values. Coins, made of metal, didn't break easily and were easy to carry.

This new kind of money quickly became popular. Coins were strong and their value could be determined by their weight and material. This made trading more fair and reliable, and people no longer needed to carry heavy seashells or other bulky items for trading.

The best part was that coins had a fixed value. This made it easier to compare the prices of different things and made trading more fair and clear. This fair way of trading helped the economy grow.

For example,
1 gold coin = 100 silver coins = 10000 copper coins.

As time passed, coins became more complex, and some countries started using paper money. Paper money was much lighter than coins and easier to carry.

Today, people all over the world use different types of money. Some countries use coins, some use paper money, and in some places, you can even pay with a card or phone.

No matter the form, money is a tool that helps people trade. It allows us to buy and sell things easily and get what we need.

But money doesn't just appear by itself. People have to work to earn money. For example, parents go to work, and their boss gives them money as a reward for their work.

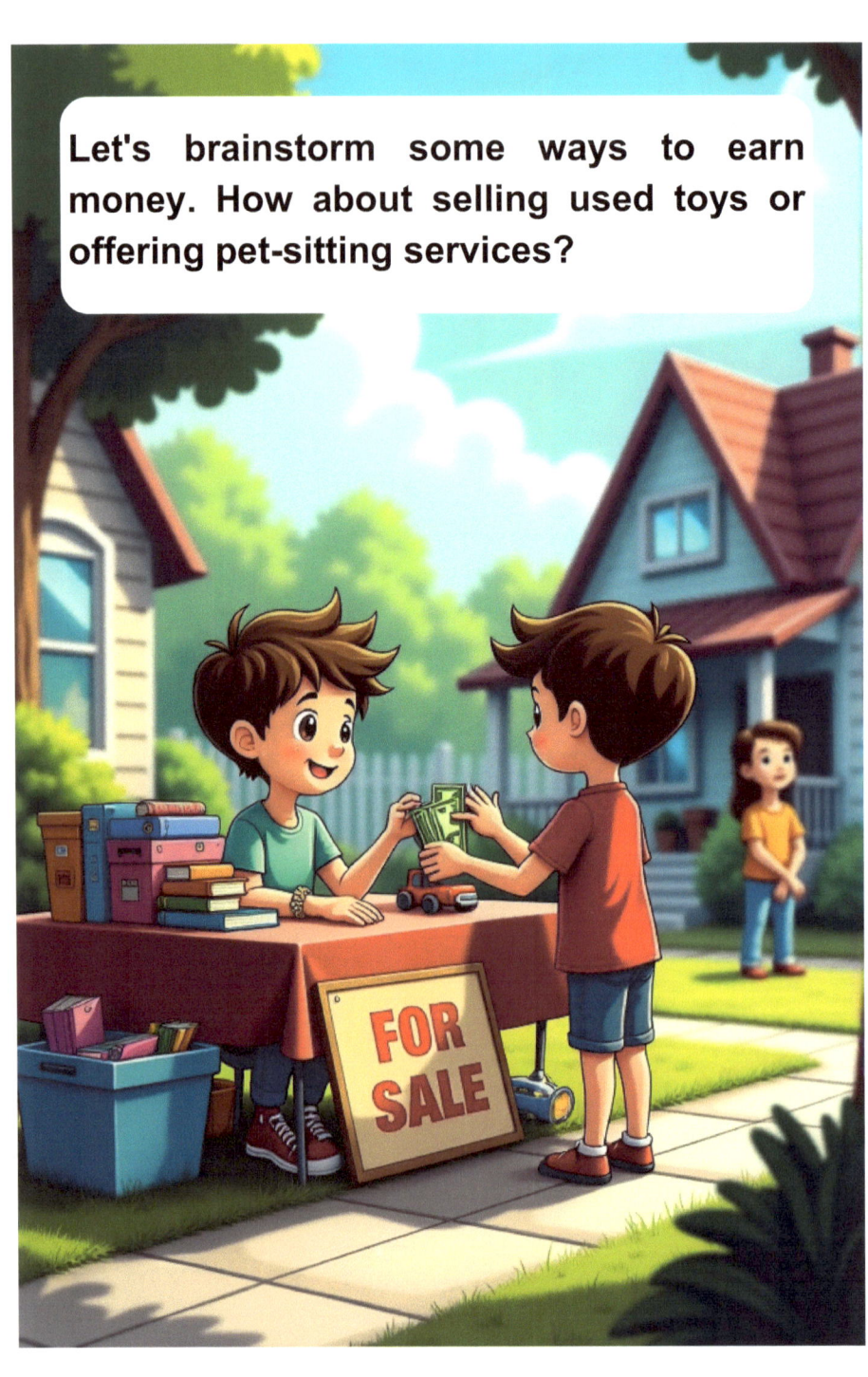

When you get money, you can use it to buy things you like, like toys or books. But before spending it, think about what you really need.

Besides spending, another important skill is "saving." Saving means putting aside some of your money to use later when you really need it.

If you want to buy something expensive, like a bicycle, saving is a good idea. By saving a little bit each time, you can eventually have enough to buy it.

Did you know? Some things might seem cheap but aren't very good, while other things are more expensive but last a long time and are worth the money. That's why it's important to understand the difference between "cheap" and "expensive."

Money isn't just for buying things. Many people use their money to help others, like donating to people in need or supporting charities.

Money is also a responsibility. Managing your money well is very important, so you'll have enough to buy what's important when you need it.

If you want to learn how to manage money, you can talk to your family and make plans together. Saving and planning will help you make smart decisions in the future.

Did you know that different countries have their own money? When traveling to other countries, we need to exchange our money for the local currency so we can buy things there.

No matter if it's coins, paper money, or paying with a card or phone, money has the same job – it helps us get what we need, and it helps us save and plan for the future.

Now, think about it – do you know where money comes from? Money isn't just a tool for trading, it also helps us manage our lives better.

Next time you see money, think about its history and importance. Whether it's ancient seashells or today's coins and bills, money is a clever invention.

The most important thing is to learn how to use money wisely, save it, and make plans. This way, you'll make smart choices, not just for today, but for the future.

Now, go tell your family and friends what you've learned! You know a lot about money now, and you'll surely become a money-smart kid in the future!

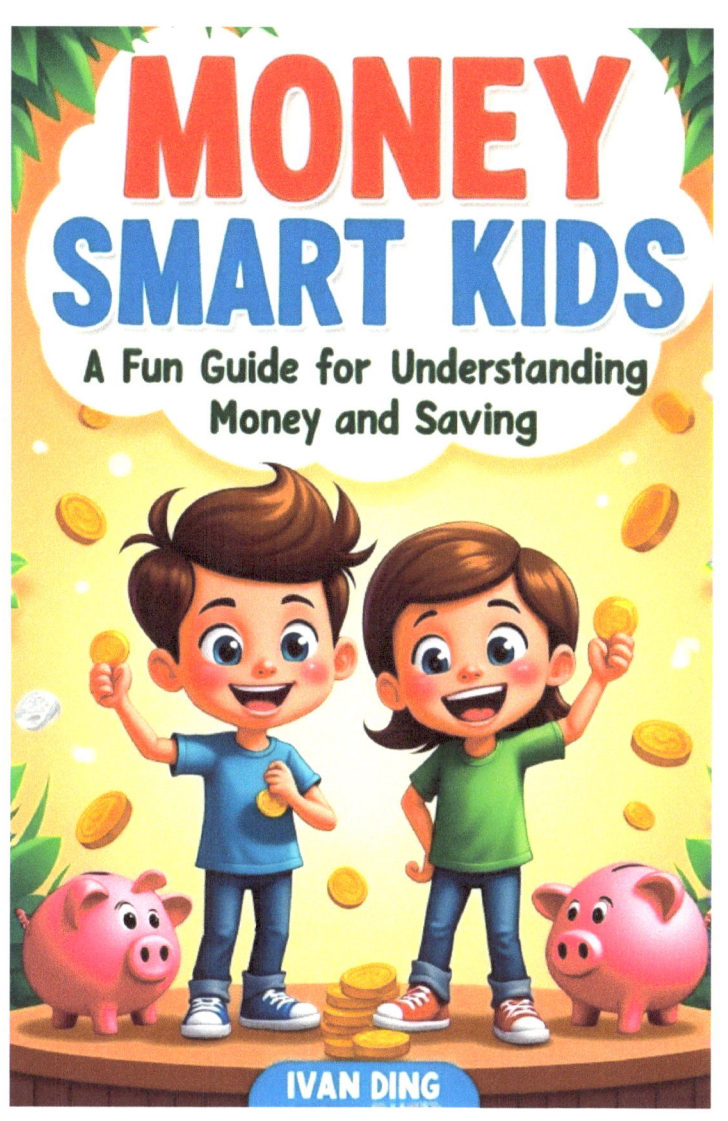

Copyright © 2024 Ivan Ding
All rights reserved.

ISBN:9798339759676

www.ingramcontent.com/pod-product-compliance
Lightning Source LLC
Chambersburg PA
CBHW041949240526

45473CB00036B/2794